Writing Skills   Contents

Weekly Units

Unit 1	Fishy tales	2
Unit 2	At the beach	3
Unit 3	The three donkeys	4
Unit 4	Alphabet soup	6
Unit 5	Addresses and postcards	7
Unit 6	The go-kart race	10
Unit 7	Days of the week	12
Unit 8	Writing nonfiction	14
Unit 9	Rhyming words	15
Unit 10	The Wind and the Sun: a play	17
Unit 11	The Wind and the Sun: a fable	19
Unit 12	Colours	20
Unit 13	Parties and invitations	22
Unit 14	Cake recipe	24
Unit 15	Anansi the spider	27
Unit 16	Yesteryear	30
Unit 17	Happy and sad	33
Unit 18	In the future...	35
Unit 19	Book Week	37
Unit 20	Characters	39
Unit 21	Me, myself and I	41
Unit 22	Monsters	44
Unit 23	The abominable snowman	46
Unit 24	Monster Meeting!	48
Unit 25	Cloud watching	49
Unit 26	Monster verbs	50
Unit 27	The chatty tortoise	52
Unit 28	Toys at midnight	54
Unit 29	Character boxes	56
Unit 30	Jack and the Beanstalk	58
Unit 31	Alice down the rabbit hole	62
Unit 32	Animal chatter	66
Unit 33	Instead of *said*	68
Unit 34	The enormous turnip	71
Unit 35	Dinosaur names	74
Unit 36	Ice-cream sundaes	76
I am a writer	My favourite story	80

With thanks to Becky Miles, Susan Purcell and Elaine Wilkinson.

UNIT 1: Writing Skills   Fishy tales

What do you think? How should the story end?

UNIT 4: Writing Skills Alphabet soup

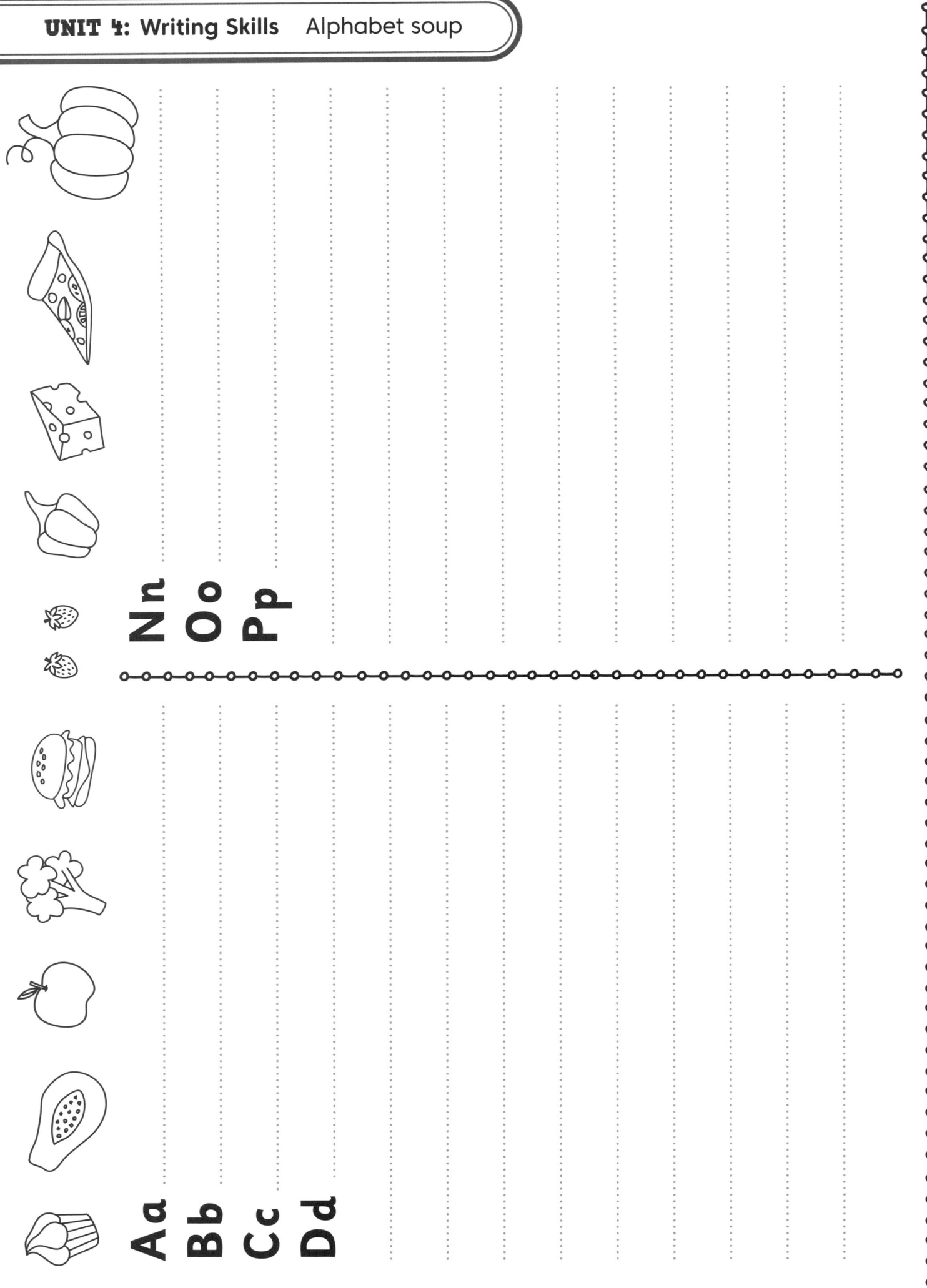

UNIT 5: Writing Skills   Addresses and postcards

UNIT 5: Writing Skills　　Addresses and postcards

Make up some names and addresses and write them here.

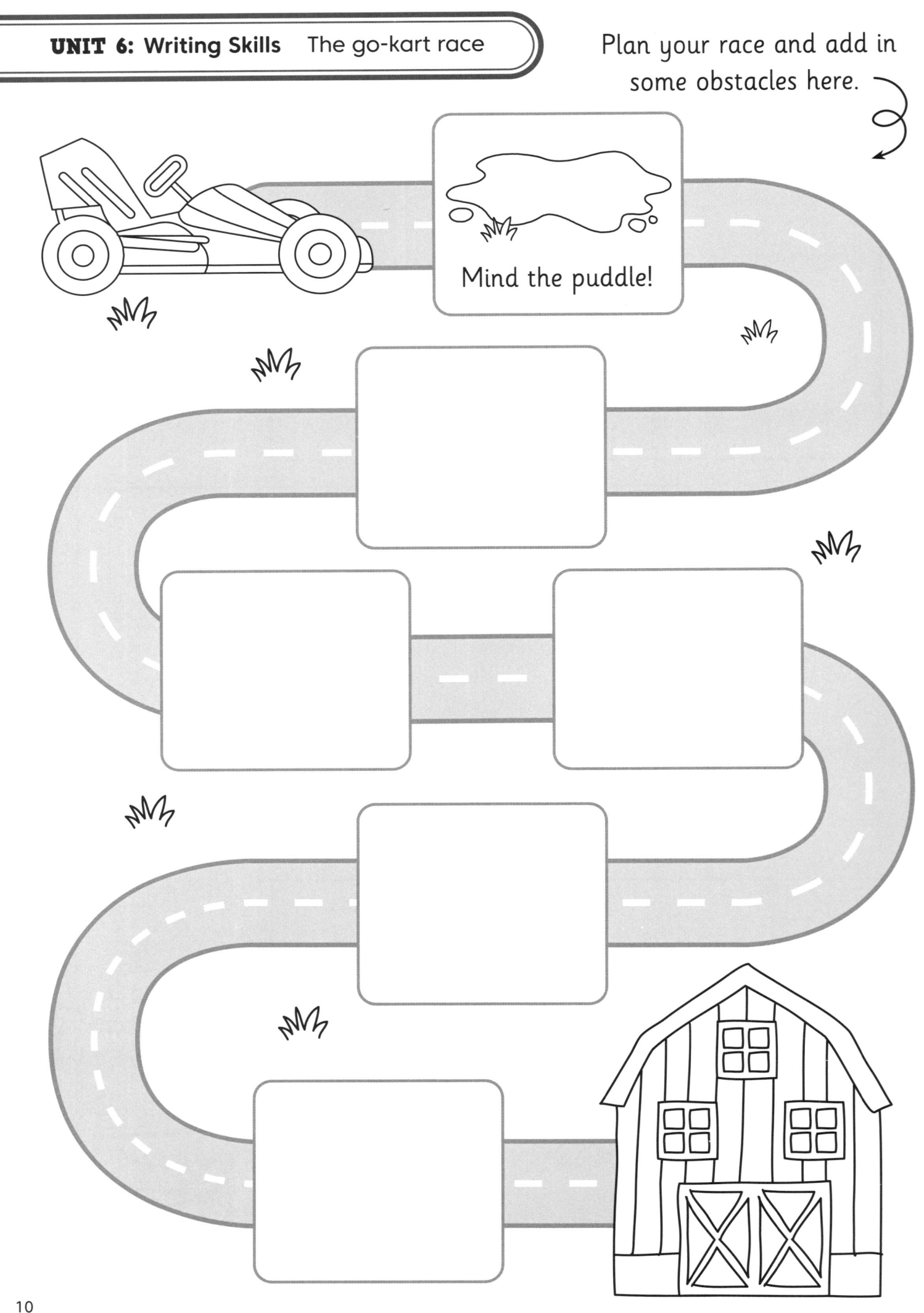

Write about the race here.

UNIT 7: Writing Skills   Days of the week

Monday

Monday

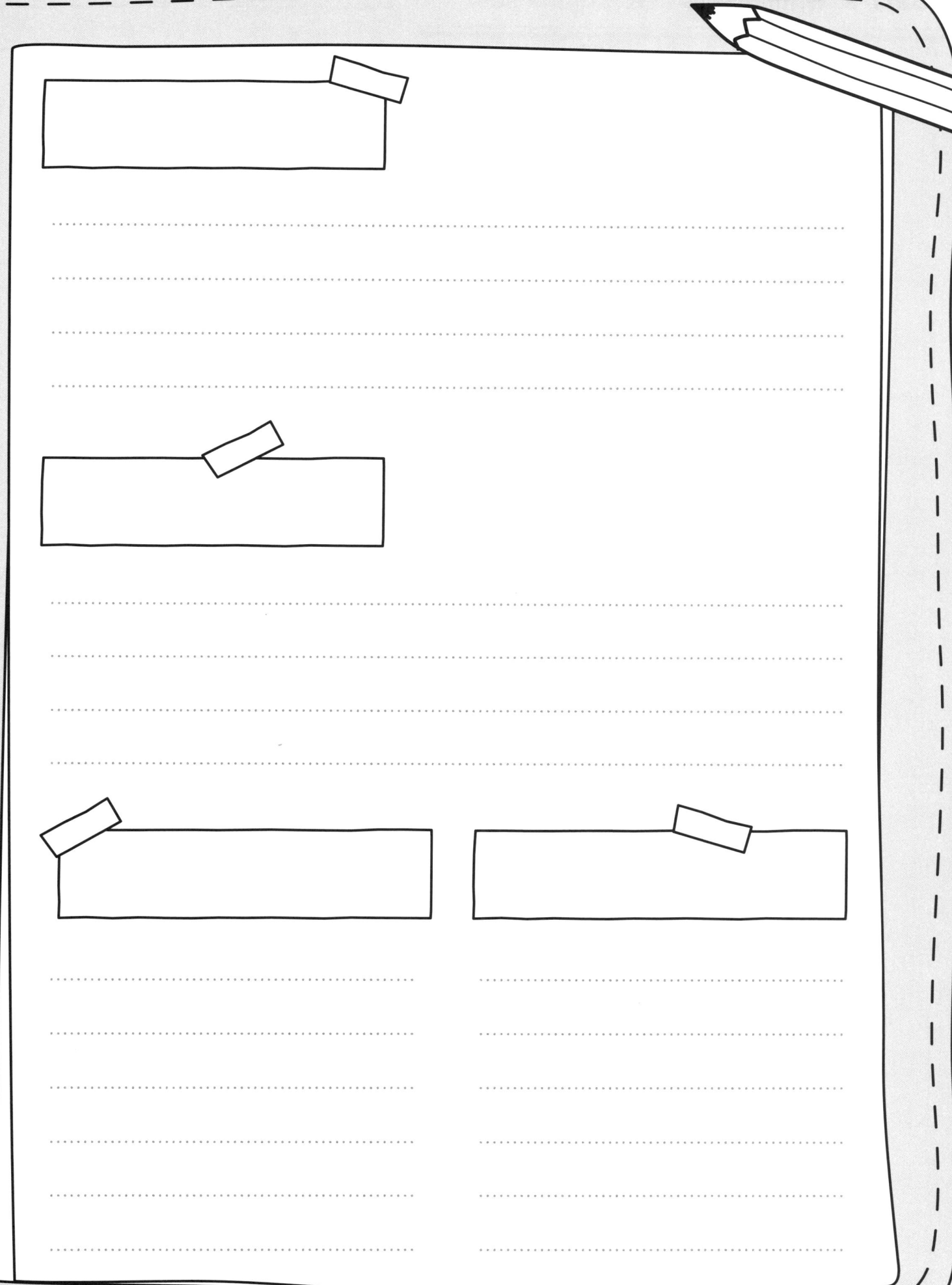

UNIT 8: Writing Skills — Writing nonfiction

Draw your bird picture here.

UNIT 9: Writing Skills   Rhyming words

Copy the rhymes about Snake, Inky and Bee here.

....
....
....
....
....

....
....
....
....
....

....
....
....
....
....

Try your own rhymes on the next page.

UNIT 9: Writing Skills   Rhyming words

Draw a picture of one of your animals.

UNIT 10: Writing Skills   The Wind and the Sun: a play

Draw a person wearing a big coat.

UNIT 10: Writing Skills — The Wind and the Sun: a play

Draw the person carrying their coat.

UNIT 11: Writing Skills   The Wind and the Sun: a fable

UNIT 12: Writing Skills   Colours

Colour the ink splat to match the colour you're writing about.

Write your colour poems here.

UNIT 13: Writing Skills   Parties and invitations

To ....

You are invited to

....

Date: ....
Time: ....
Place: ....

From ....

Write about the party here.

UNIT 14: Writing Skills   Cake recipe

Write your cake ingredients here.

With a grown-up's help, turn on the oven to 200°C (400°F) to let it heat up.

UNIT 14: Writing Skills — Cake recipe

Don't forget to leave the cake(s) to cool!

UNIT 15: Writing Skills   Anansi the spider

Draw Anansi's route to the melon,
then plan and write your story over the page.

UNIT 15: Writing Skills — Anansi the spider

UNIT 16: Writing Skills Yesteryear

Carry on writing over the page.

UNIT 16: Writing Skills — Yesteryear

UNIT 17: Writing Skills   Happy and sad

What makes you happy?

UNIT 17: Writing Skills   Happy and sad

What makes you sad?

UNIT 18: Writing Skills In the future...

What will you look like in the future?

UNIT 18: Writing Skills — In the future...

Draw where you will live in the future.

UNIT 19: Writing Skills   Book Week

UNIT 19: Writing Skills   Book Week

UNIT 20: Writing Skills   Characters

Carry on writing over the page.

UNIT 20: Writing Skills — Characters

UNIT 21: Writing Skills   Me, myself and I

Write about yourself here.

UNIT 22: Writing Skills Monsters

Draw your monster here.

Write your monster's name here.

UNIT 23: Writing Skills — The abominable snowman

UNIT 24: Writing Skills — Monster Meeting!

UNIT 25: Writing Skills   Cloud watching

C
L
O
U
D
S

UNIT 26: Writing Skills   Monster verbs

Write your rhyming words here.

Try a rhyming sentence here.

UNIT 27: Writing Skills   The chatty tortoise

UNIT 28: Writing Skills — Toys at midnight

Don't forget a story has a beginning, a middle and an end.

UNIT 29: Writing Skills — Character boxes

UNIT 30: Writing Skills — Jack and the Beanstalk

Use this page to plan your story.

Carry on writing over the page.

UNIT 30: Writing Skills Jack and the Beanstalk

UNIT 31: Writing Skills — Alice down the rabbit hole

Don't forget a story has a beginning, a middle and an end.

UNIT 31: Writing Skills — Alice down the rabbit hole

Write your rhyming sentences here.

UNIT 33: Writing Skills — Instead of *said*

Write **how** a person said something here.

Use the words above in sentences here.

UNIT 33: Writing Skills — Instead of *said*

Try writing a story using one of your sentences.

UNIT 34: Writing Skills   The enormous turnip

UNIT 34: Writing Skills   The enormous turnip

UNIT 35: Writing Skills Dinosaur names

UNIT 36: Writing Skills   Ice-cream sundaes

I AM A WRITER — My favourite story

Write and illustrate your favourite story here.